E
Osb   Osborn, Lois
          My Dad is really some-
          thing

          #9.08

DATE DUE		
FE 15 '88	JY 11 '91	NO 02 '06
MR 3 '88	JY 1 '93	SE 25 '08
AG 3 '88		
AG 9 '88	JY 27 '93	JE 03
Fe 20 '	MAY 19 '94	OC 27 '12
JY 11 '89	MAY 28 '94	
AG 31 '89	JUL 7 '94	
MR 6 '90	MR 25	JE 29 '17
AP 25 '90	JUL 15 '98	
JY 31 '90	MAY 14	
OC 11 '90	MR 03	
JA 16 '91	NOV 22 '99	
JA 31 '9	SE 25 '01	

MEDIALOG
Alexandria, Ky 41001

My Dad Is Really Something

Lois Osborn   *pictures by* Rodney Pate

ALBERT WHITMAN & COMPANY, NILES, ILLINOIS

Text © 1983 by Lois Osborn
Illustrations © 1983 by Rodney Pate
Published in 1983 by Albert Whitman & Company, Niles, Illinois
Published simultaneously in Canada by
General Publishing, Limited, Toronto
12   11   10   9   8   7   6   5   4   3

The text of this book is set in fourteen point Fairfield.

Library of Congress Cataloging in Publication Data

Osborn, Lois.
  My dad is really something.

  (Concept book. Level 1)
  Summary: When they compare fathers, Harry finds that
his father just doesn't stack up against his friend
Ron's father, until he finds out that Ron is
describing a fantasy.
  [1. Fathers and sons—Fiction] I. Pate, Rodney,
ill. II. Title. III. Series.
PZ7.O797MZ 1983   [E]   83-1292
ISBN 0-8075-5329-8 (lib. bdg.)

Dedicated to the memory of my own father, Ralph Page Judd. L.O.
To Kenny and especially Mom. R.P.

Ron is a new boy in my class.
I like him a lot.
But sometimes he makes me mad.

One day I showed the kids at school a book
my dad had written.
Then Ron had to speak up.

"Aw, that's nothing, Harry George," he said.
"You should only see what *my* father can do.
He can tear a phone book in half with his bare hands.
I bet *your* father can't do that."

When I got home, I gave the phone book to my dad.
I told him what Ron's father could do.
"How about you?" I asked.
He shook his head.
"I'm no strong man, Harry George," he said.
I put the phone book away.
He could at least have tried.

Then I remembered how once
my mom and I had watched my dad
climb a tall ladder,

crawl up a steep roof,

hang onto a chimney with one arm,

and reach way out to rescue my kitten.
We were scared my dad would fall.

Maybe my dad isn't real strong,
but he sure is brave. So I told Ron all about
what my dad had done.

"Aw that's nothing, Harry George," Ron said.
"My father fought in the war.
He rescued wounded soldiers.
He has a whole box full of medals he won
for bravery."

After school, I watched my dad fix my bike.
I looked at all the tools in his box.
I wished they were medals.
"How come you never fought in the war?"
I asked my dad.
"Flat feet and poor eyesight," my dad said.
"They couldn't use me. I was lucky."

"Lucky?" I exclaimed. "*Lucky*? You could've
won a lot of medals, like Ron's father."
"Ron's father?" my dad said. "Oh, I remember him.
The fellow who tears up telephone books.
So he won medals, did he?"

"For bravery," I explained.

"Well, good for him," said my dad,
and he shut his toolbox with a bang.

For my birthday, my dad bought me a soccer ball.
"It's just like the ones the pros use," I told Ron.

"Aw, that's nothing, Harry George," he said.
"My father gave me his very own football.
The one he had in college. Once he carried that ball
eighty-five yards for a touchdown and won the game!"

I wondered why my dad never played football.
He doesn't even watch it on TV.
When I got home I said to him, "Can flat feet
and poor eyesight keep you from playing football?"
"I don't know," he replied,
"but being short and fat sure can."

My dad is short and fat.

Later, my dad and I finished the model plane
we had been working on.
I could hardly wait to show it to Ron.
"See what my dad and I made?" I said to him.
"I bet you and your father never made anything like this."

"Aw, that's nothing, Harry George," Ron answered.
"My father doesn't fool around with *model* planes.
He flies *real* ones instead.
The kind that take off and land on a carrier.
That's dangerous stuff!"

As soon as I got home, I asked my dad
if he would like to be a pilot.
"I don't care that much about flying," he told me.
"Why not?" I asked.
"Well, let's just say I feel better getting off a plane
than I do getting on."
I wished he hadn't said that.
I started to walk away.
"Wait a minute," said my dad.
"Does Ron's father happen to be an airline pilot?"
"Oh no," I replied. "He flies fighter jets.
On carriers. For the Navy."

"That figures," I heard my dad mutter.

The next evening, we had an open house at school.
My mom and dad came.
They looked at my work and talked to my teacher.
"Is Ron's father here?" my dad asked her.
"Harry George tells me he's quite a guy.
I'd like to meet him."
My teacher looked at me in surprise.
"You must be thinking of someone else," she said.
"Ron's father died years ago."

I walked home like a robot.
I couldn't talk or think.

My mom and dad and I sat around
the kitchen table having a snack.
I didn't feel much like eating.
"How could Ron do that to me?" I asked.
"We were friends. Why did he have to lie to me?"
"Maybe it didn't seem like lying to Ron,"
my dad suggested.

"All that junk about
tearing the telephone book," I said.
"*And* the medals. *And* football.
And flying a plane.
All lies!" I went on.
"And I believed him. He fooled me.
I can never be friends with him again. Never!"

"Don't be too hard on him," my mom said.
"Ron doesn't have a father, so he made one up."

I didn't want to talk about Ron anymore.
I didn't even say goodnight.
I just turned my back and walked out of the kitchen.
I had a good work-out with my punching bag.
After that I felt better and went to bed.

I lay there thinking how different
school was going to be without Ron.
No more borrowing his mystery books, either.
I'd miss opening my desk and finding
one of those silly cartoons he likes to draw.
Nobody else I know could invent a father
who would tear up phone books, win football games,
fly fighter jets, and win medals.

Then I remembered how I had wished
my dad could do all those things.
I didn't feel very good about that.
I wondered what it would be like to have
a make-believe father instead of a real dad like mine.

I'm glad my dad is real.

The next morning I told my dad that maybe
I'd be friends with Ron after all.
He smiled and put his arm around me.
I asked him if Ron could go fishing with us sometime.
"Sure," said my dad. "Let's make it next weekend."

That's how the three of us began doing things together.

At recess today, I heard Ron say to some kids,
"Harry George's father takes us fishing.
We go sailing, too.
And he knows ten different ways to make paper airplanes.
Harry George's father is really something."

Yep, that's my dad, all right.
He is really something!